My Neighborhood
The Library

Aaron Carr

www.av2books.com

LET'S READ
AV²
BY WEIGL™
ADDED VALUE · AUDIO VISUAL

Go to **www.av2books.com**, and enter this book's unique code.

BOOK CODE

U 5 2 5 0

AV² by Weigl brings you media enhanced books that support active learning.

AV² provides enriched content that supplements and complements this book. Weigl's AV² books strive to create inspired learning and engage young minds in a total learning experience.

Your AV² Media Enhanced books come alive with...

Audio
Listen to sections of the book read aloud.

Video
Watch informative video clips.

Embedded Weblinks
Gain additional information for research.

Try This!
Complete activities and hands-on experiments.

Key Words
Study vocabulary, and complete a matching word activity.

Quizzes
Test your knowledge.

Slide Show
View images and captions, and prepare a presentation.

... and much, much more!

Published by AV² by Weigl
350 5th Avenue, 59th Floor New York, NY 10118
Website: www.av2books.com   www.weigl.com

Library of Congress Cataloging-in-Publication Data

Carr, Aaron.
 The library / Aaron Carr.
    pages cm. -- (My neighborhood)
 ISBN 978-1-62127-346-2 (hardcover) -- ISBN 978-1-62127-351-6 (softcover)
 1. Libraries--Juvenile literature. 2. Librarians--Juvenile literature. I. Title.
 Z665.5.C37 2014
 027--dc23
                                              2013006709.

Printed in the United States of America in North Mankato, Minnesota
1 2 3 4 5 6 7 8 9 0 17 16 15 14 13

032013
WEP300113

Project Coordinators: Heather Kissock and Megan Cuthbert Design: Mandy Christiansen

Weigl acknowledges Getty Images as the primary image supplier for this title.

The Library

CONTENTS

This is my neighborhood.

The library is in my neighborhood.

5

The library has many different books and movies.

I can choose the books and movies that I want to borrow from the library.

I go to the librarian when I want to take a book home.

8

The librarian also helps me find things in the library.

9

Authors W

One part of the library is filled with the books I like to read.

There are also toys
that I can play with.

Begin to Read

Folk

I can go to the library to use a computer.

I use computers to learn new things.

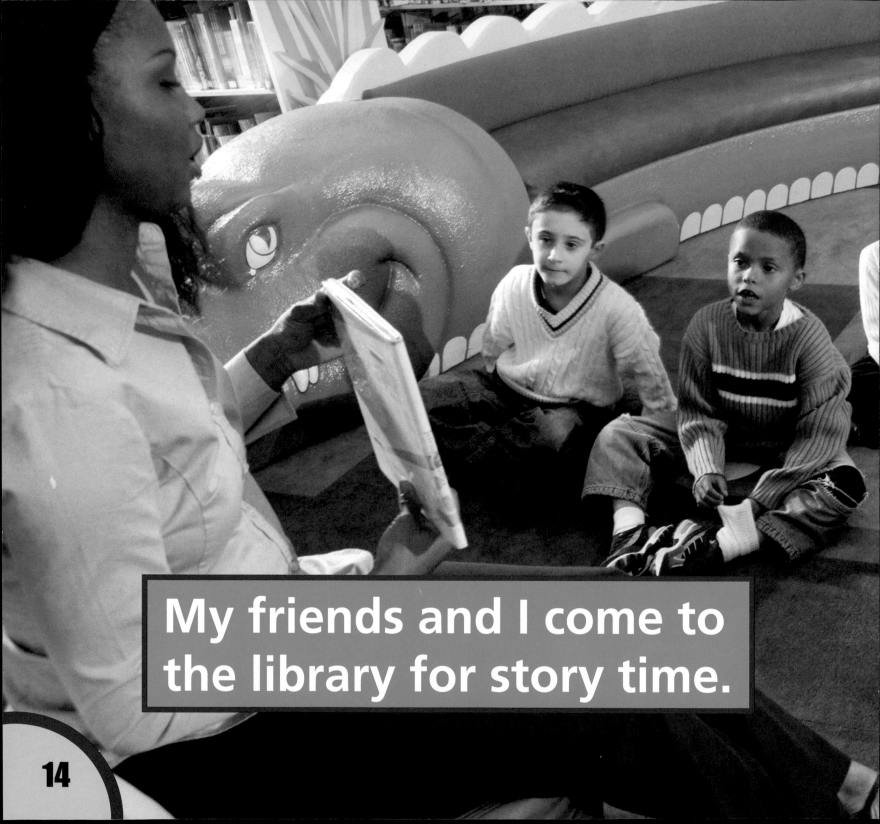

My friends and I come to the library for story time.

14

We listen to the librarian read books out loud.

People in my neighborhood meet at the library to take classes.

I can join a club at the library and read books with my friends.

17

I can visit the library with my class from school.

My friends and I learn about new books and play on the computer.

19

I often see librarians in my neighborhood.

Sometimes they hold puppet shows and book fairs.

See what you have learned about libraries and librarians.

Which of these pictures does not show a library?

KEY WORDS

Research has shown that as much as 65 percent of all written material published in English is made up of 300 words. These 300 words cannot be taught using pictures or learned by sounding them out. They must be recognized by sight. This book contains 54 common sight words to help young readers improve their reading fluency and comprehension. This book also teaches young readers several important content words, such as proper nouns. These words are paired with pictures to aid in learning and improve understanding.

Page	Sight Words First Appearance
4	is, my, this
5	in, the
6	and, books, different, has, many
7	can, from, I, that, to, want
8	a, go, home, take, want, when
9	also, find, helps, me, things
10	like, one, of, part, read, with
11	are, play, there
12	use
13	learn, new
14	come, for, story, time
15	out, we
16	at, people
18	school
19	about, on
20	often, see
21	sometimes, they

Page	Content Words First Appearance
4	neighborhood
5	library
6	movies
8	librarian
11	toys
12	computer
14	friends
16	classes
17	club
21	puppet shows, book fairs

24